with love

Isabelle Fernandes

1

THE THREE-LEAF CLOVER

Isabelle Fernandez

The Three-leaf Clover

Illustrated by the author

ISBN 978-1-717-74158-5
Amazon.com

Once upon a time in the countryside, there was a beautiful green meadow. It extended as far as the eye could see. Its vibrant green color delighted all visitors who were lucky enough to happen by.

Upon closer inspection, you could see that the meadow was mainly populated with grass and clover. A few clovers had four leaves, but most of them had three.

One day, an unusual conversation took place between two clovers. A curious young three-leaf clover turned to his neighbor, a four-leaf clover and asked:

"Could you tell me how it feels to have four leaves instead of three?"

"It's an experience you can't even begin to comprehend. I feel so handsome, so complete, and so loved! I feel special. For me, being here on earth is like being in paradise every single day."

After a long silence, the four-leaf clover returned the question.

"And you, how do you feel? What is it like having only three leaves?"

"I must say that I do not particularly feel special... there are so many three-leaf clovers! One more, one less, what difference does it make?"

"You are right, said the four-leaf clover smugly, and when people come looking for us they don't even pay attention to you. They look for four-leaf clovers like me!"

Totally absorbed in his own thoughts he added:

"I can only imagine the day someone finally spots me and I can bring them luck!"

At this point, the three-leaf clover imperceptibly started wilting.

"You are right! What a beautiful goal in life! As for me, I don't really know my own purpose. No one looks at me, no one wants to pick me... no one loves me, nor is anyone hoping to love me someday. I feel so depressed suddenly!"

Nearby, a particularly shiny blade of grass was finishing his morning meditation.

"Good morning young man! What bad news is upsetting you so much?"

"I am depressed. I am nothing special. I wish I could bring luck or happiness to someone."

Because the blade of grass was too wise to cast judgment upon the three-leaf clover's perspective on things, he left him alone facing his predicament. Surrounding him with compassion he whispered:

"Welcome, feel, and release... welcome, feel, and release..."

Sinking deep into his obsessive thoughts, the young three-leaf clover kept mumbling in a low voice:

"I wish so much I was a four-leaf clover! But I only have three leaves. Maybe I can find a fourth one somewhere..."

That very evening, a ferocious storm spread over the meadow, and everyone was forced to endure the unrelenting wind and the driving rain.

Faced with this abundance of rain and wind, the three-leaf clover began to believe his final hour had come. "It might not be so bad" he rationalized. He would finally be free of the bad luck that had cursed him from birth.

In all this mess, one blade of grass, the shiny blade of grass, managed to stay proudly standing throughout the climatic event. He would swing back and forth to the rhythm of the gusts.

During a brief respite between two water drop bombardments, the three-leaf clover noticed him. "How graceful and elegant his stem is! It is so aerodynamic!"

Then he quickly glanced in the opposite direction and saw the four-leaf clover struggling as much as he was. He realized that having a fourth leaf made it harder to fight against the element. But he still believed it was well worth this temporary inconvenience.

At sunrise, the meadow had transformed into a battlefield. Here and there, leaves lay on the ground, and dismembered clovers were crying over their losses.

For the blades of grass, things seemed to be better. They were already stripped of their water drops, and some of them even featured a flower bud popping out at the top of their hairdo.

Much to his disappointment, the three-leaf clover noticed that he had survived the dreadful night without a single scratch or bruise. Many were not so lucky. Then, he noticed it. At his feet laid a single leaf, similar to one of his own.

Suddenly, his wish from the previous evening jumped back into his mind. He considered the possibility of grabbing the fallen leaf and instantly turning himself into a four-leaf clover. He would have to be careful that no one saw him, or his peers might uncover his charade.

Too late! As if he had read his mind, his neighbor, another three-leaf clover grabbed the magical leaf, and gloriously positioned it at the base of his own trio.

The sun started shining with its thousand rays warming up the reviving meadow. Unfortunately, the three-leaf clover's heart didn't warm up accordingly.

It was Saturday. This meant that the nearby roads would be jammed with traffic and that many humans would wander into the meadow. They would search everywhere for the four-leaf clovers and pick them with great delight.

The four-leaf clover could already hear the screams of joy and victory around him.

"Here is one! Got a four-leaf clover! I am so lucky! This is going to be the greatest weekend ever!"

While fantasizing about this kind of encounter, the four-leaf clover was busy making himself look all-fancy.

Oblivious to the unfolding drama around him, the shiny blade of grass was going through his own transformation. It was a life-changing event, and it required no help from anyone. He was giving birth or rather he was witnessing the birth of the creamy flowers perched at the top of his blade.

Indeed, he was making no effort other than allowing this life energy to manifest through him. It was a solemn moment, one that the blade of grass had lived repeatedly, and that he always welcomed with a deep sense of marvel. He never tired of watching this gift of life and the sacred blooming it created. He welled with joy and ineffable happiness.

He felt like shouting to express his joy to the world, but he was far too wise to give in to this temptation his ego was whispering.

"That your will be done… that your will be done…" he said again and again.

Wanting to be discrete, from the corner of his eye, the three-leaf clover saw the feather of creamy flowers open and fluff in the air. This bunch of little bland colored flowers didn't look like much! Even less when you compared them to the poppies that had bloomed a few months prior not far from there.

"Ha! Those poppies had a good reason to feel proud. Those beautiful bright red petals…! That was a real show, a real accomplishment!

On the other hand, those weird brooms that were sticking out the blade of grass just had nothing going for them. But because the three-leaf clover liked the shiny blade of grass, he didn't say anything and just turned away.

It was now time for that special moment that one of the clovers dreaded so much and the other looked so forward to. Snip, snip! The four-leaf clover and the fake four-leaf clover were both grabbed very delicately by fingers that shook with excitement.

Left abandoned, the three-leaf clover was already wallowing in self-pity when something hit his head. It was a dried little leaf falling back down from the skies. He thought it looked familiar. Then, there was a second hit, a stronger one. It was his neighbor, the fake four-leaf clover, now naked and uprooted...

Upon seeing this, something suddenly unlocked inside his heart. The three-leaf clover felt a myriad of emotions springing forth. He became overwhelmed and found himself floating for a moment in an inner world he knew very little about. He went from feeling pity to relief and finally to a surprising new feeling: thankfulness.

This is when the three-leaf clover had an epiphany. Although he still didn't know his goal in life, he was simply thankful he was alive.

He took his first conscious deep and long breath. As his lungs filled with air, he discovered the pleasure of feeling the oxygen flowing in and out of his leaves. He could also feel each cell of his body come alive like never before.

He had a loving smile for the real four-leaf clover that had just sacrificed his life for a human's happiness. Any trace of jealousy had evaporated.

Then, he had a thought of compassion for the fake four-leaf clover. Although he only had three leaves, that clover had actually brought him luck!

The young three-leaf clover felt lighter than ever. He wanted to jump, dance, and shout to the world how happy he was to be alive. But maybe he had become too wise to give in to this temptation his ego was whispering.

The three-leaf clover felt his heart swell and thought it was going to explode. He noticed his three beautiful green leaves were illuminated from the inside by a bright light... a shiny light... just like his friend's, the blade of grass!

He turned towards the blade of grass hoping to catch his glance. Maybe it would be okay to share his joy just with him.

As if he had read his mind, the blade of grass who was indeed looking at him, had the shiniest smile on his face. He winked at him before retreating to his evening meditation. The three-leaf clover thought he faintly heard:

"Peace, love and gratitude... peace, love and gratitude..." and then he peacefully fell asleep.

The next morning, the three-leaf clover woke up to a new perfumed smell around him. He immediately knew where it came from. His friend the blade of grass was busy dusting his feather of flowers so the seeds could be freed and gently be blown away by the wind.

"Your children are beautiful", exclaimed the three-leaf clover to his new friend with true admiration.

Although the night before he had been blind to the beauty in that feathery flower, this morning, the three-leaf clover truly perceived things very differently.

Everything around him had become beautiful, interesting, deep, unique and special... special, yes.

He remembered the four-leaf clover saying he was special because of his fourth leaf. If he had still been alive, knowing better now, he would have told him that everything is special in its own way.

"And, if we are all special, being special is not special in itself! It also means that it is normal to be special."

This was good news!

"The key is to find what is special in each of us," he concluded with immense satisfaction. "Sometimes it is easy to discover, as in the case of the four-leaf clover, and sometimes it is more subtle. The fake four-leaf clover never got to find out what made him special. He was looking at others to imitate them. Like I do."

This new awareness made him feel a bit ashamed.

A voice brought him back down to earth. The blade of grass was busy with his precious charge. Philosophically he explained:

"I am putting them in the hands of destiny. It is now their turn to settle somewhere else and live as best they can this adventure called life."

Listening to him talk, the young three-leaf clover couldn't resist thinking:

"If there really was someone more special than all others, it wouldn't be the four-leaf clover, it would be him, this simple blade of grass right here!"

"Loving yourself and what happens to you, these are the secrets of life!" he exclaimed out loud inspired by the words of his neighbor.

And although he hadn't grown one inch since the day before, the three-leaf clover suddenly felt taller than ever.

About the author

Isabelle Fernandez is a life coach and author who enjoys writing inspiring stories for all ages. Her tales invite us to take a look inside ourselves, to listen to our soul and to wonder about our personal role in a world in transition.

To share about the book, you can contact the author directly on her Facebook page:

www.facebook.com/the3leafclover

For information regarding life coaching or ADHD coaching, you can go to the author's coaching website:

www.mycoachisabelle.com

85165489R00029

Made in the USA
San Bernardino, CA
18 August 2018